BOOKS BY UCHE NDUKA

Living in Public (Writers Collective of Kristiania Inc, 2018)
Sageberry 1 (AMAB Books, 2017)
Nine East (SPM publications, 2013)
Ijele (Overpass Books, 2012)
eel on reef (Akashic Books, 2007)
Heart's Field (Yeti Press, 2005)
If Only The Night (Sojourner Press, 2002)
Belltime Letters (NewLeaf Press, 2000)
The Bremen Poems (Yeti Press, 1999)
Chiaroscuro (Yeti Press, 1997)
Second Act (Jounoblues Communications Ltd, 1994)
Flower Child (Update Communications, 1988)

FACING YOU

CITY LIGHTS SPOTLIGHT SERIES NO. 19

UCHE NDUKA

FACING YOU

POEMS

CITY LIGHTS

SAN FRANCISCO

CITY LIGHTS SPOTLIGHT
The City Lights Spotlight Series was founded in 2009,
and is edited by Garrett Caples.

Library of Congress Cataloging-in-Publication Data
Title: Facing you : poems / Uche Nduka.
Description: San Francisco : City Lights, 2020. | Series: City Lights
Spotlight series ; no. 19
Identifiers: LCCN 2019053008 | ISBN 9780872868304 (trade paperback)
Subjects: LCGFT: Poetry.
Classification: LCC PR9387.9.N373 F33 2020 | DDC 821/.914—dc23
LC record available at https://lccn.loc.gov/2019053008

Cover art: Copyright © 2008 by Katerina Pinosova
Cover image: *Applegals and Wild Apple Tree* [detail], 2008, acrylic ink
and pastel on paper, 70 x 100 cm.
Her work can be found at katerinapinosova.com.
The editor would like to thank Brian Lucas, Joyelle McSweeney, and
Katerina Pinosova for assistance with this project.

All City Lights Books are distributed to the trade by
Consortium Book Sales and Distribution: www.cbsd.com

For small press poetry titles by this author and others,
visit Small Press Distribution: www.spdbooks.com

City Lights Books are published at the City Lights Bookstore,
261 Columbus Avenue, San Francisco, CA 94133
www.citylights.com

CONTENTS

FACING YOU

KICK OFF YOUR SHOES

A man you can't reach
is not the man I am.
Never the same twice
I have no guile at
             my command.

             I keep nothing
in reserve. Kick off your
shoes and I will
show you that partiality
                 is perpetual

on the cutting room floor
on the casting couch.

DIRTY TRICKS

The day I nosed
my way into the world
was the day Edith Piaf left it.

It was as starry
as all the dirty tricks of God.

Suits, counter-suits.
Shadows that walked
Away with silver sheath.

Between two trees
Someone held up a sign.

Seeing the mind crucified.
Falling between two chairs.

Lip-line half-lit.
A trawler's undone.

Oliveleaf cloverleaf
coming at us.

BRING THE NOTES

Dumbass thrice underlined.
When shall it be? Bring
The notes. Far-flung slats.
Letters to the void. Blackout
In the foyer & the climb
Of her violins. If you hold on
To the tail of a word. A voyage
you created for us to disappear into.
To let them revolve; to fill
This solitude with marvelous things.
Starlight on cheese. Cellos looking
for lost watches. What's your
speed limit when you ride a stanza?

IN ANOTHER DIRECTION

What is found
in the wilderness
knows you.

If ever he is
In the room.

The country
is not yet running
out of beanbags.

In another direction
a fever is a prompt.

This country
is not yet running
out of bearhugs.

TIGHTNESS OF BLUE

Turkey breast & ANA REVIEW.
Ash-grey brush cut. How to brave
a twilight.   Trashcan,
glowworm & mortal mush   It's
becoming more difficult
to expound upon intangibles.
                    This adds
to the tightness of blue
& those being left behind.
A leave-taking that is also
an arrival.   And don't
forget to take a break from gazing at me.

I HAVEN'T SEEN ENOUGH OF YOU

Must the poem
only catch me
        behaving correctly?

You came.
You came closer
to read the lines
written all over my body.

I haven't seen enough of you.
I haven't seen you enough.
I need something better than a guide.
I need someone
        I can get lost in.

PONDER THE GRIT

On this black sand
mayhem is not misdirection.
I can't take
their totalitarian logic
anymore. Don't cover
this hiatus in fellow-feeling
with mumbo-jumbo. I'm
not here to sound grand
about these Double Agents
of designer protest. Of
course obsessional grottiness
does not come into it. Ponder
the grit of the longest shot. I
don't seek immunity. I
will not be neutral with calamity.

FROM YOUR SLANT

Keep chewing gum.
These are metrics of
a meltdown. A
life of seeing and being
seen approaching 130
decibels. A surrender
to the moon kiting in the sky.
Slam the car door
and see who comes out.
Chute, talk, rosebush.
The rubble, this time.
From your slant then from
mine. Or somebody else
ambushed by a mugging.
Is the print of love
becoming too small for you to read?

LOSING MY COOL

This song is shitty
& she is courting
me & I'm losing my cool.
Nobody is overly concerned
with who is leaking
military secrets to the enemy.
Life's hard but not
so hard that she won't
get it on with me.
The rain takes out the trash.
We stand our ground.
Life's hard but not
so hard that I won't
get it on with her.

STEPPING UP

East Wall

    Starlifing

Grinder's cherry

    moving me to

        green lipstick

Scene of war
    against war

Tired of brackets
    but not
        of wild-maned words

Wherever you go
    your contours
        run true

HONOR ROLL

The vessels
appeared to be working well

that music ain't funny anymore

didn't rest
didn't muse

between two terrifying locations

drank myself to ecstasy

this is the imperfect place
to start finding out what's
in the filing cabinet of the heart
but if you need a home
come live under my cracked bone

EDGE

Still waiting
for my snack

I'm not appeased
yet I give

you access to my excess

We parachute
into

the hillside in unison

We sprint
for the magic
of the dubious world

9 INTRUSIONS

Stay cracked-up
says the moss
to you

and you
and you

in the letters
of the night

right touch
as perfect as sex
can make them
below a skiff

OVERALL MOOD

Like God on LSD.
In seven positions
her sweat fell on me
                    that morning.

On a toast in roiling mist.
The skies in her veins.

IN A TEXTILE MILL

Who really knows
    the answer
        but that light
            flashing through brown kisses

Luckily for us
    we are in the middle
        of a beautiful confusion

EXTREME WEATHER

Eye on the exit—

next to the pleasure
of watermarks on blank paper

turn me in   tuck me in

I thought you might
get a kick
out of leaning on my door

NO REPLICATION

I did speak
to the darker moments
of a sounding board

take after quick take
in the southern heights

poems in various states
of undress

I want nothing more
than to avert the indignity
of a hurried footage

those riots are chords too

POETRY

When I asked
why he was shot
on the street by a cop
they counterasked:
What does that have
to do with poetry?

MUCH LIKE FLAVOR

A porch blown apart
by white doves.

Every silly fight is me.

I have brushed
the teeth of octaves.
I can now twirl
in my desire.

THE PROVIDER

I'm not a part of this city.
I don't live in this city.
I'm this city.

Dear Blues,
          I'm not blue
                    just because
                              I sing you.

CASEIN

White light
darkening your thighs

contorted streets
contortions begging
for consequence

that's no way
to mute your peaks

a scream on a runway

LOTUS & RUBY

Cold or not
you can find it
while sober and burning your rose.

Why do I lick
your skin as if for the first time?

A silence
from which a song gushes.

Solitude of bells.

PURPLE FUR HOODIE

Despair; song-filled tenderness.
May it not be your hair alone
that is rebellious.

She gave me a hard shove
gave me a hard-on.
May it not be your thought alone
that is rebellious.

The rain shakes its fists.
Glassful of bile. Aspects of innocence.
The shadow wants to tell us something.

RATHER THAN RETREATING

I am the one
who takes the heaviness
away from your illusion.

May our small talk
not remain chaste.

There is nothing superfluous
in the placenta.
History is a bit ridiculous.

SUMMERING WITH YOU

A stuck out tongue.
A rowlock.
What can I give in return
to the milky traffic? To
live each day as if
it were my last.
Shadows write on
cut pages. Don't be
a miser in the light.

AIR AROUND A VASE

We prayed before
and after war and felt
sick about it later.

I want, if possible,
a little bit of an insane world.
I'm a sucker for toy-shops.

Tuesday fled on a boat.
Inside an azalea
is an exclamation point.

INTO THE POLLEN

Tenderness needs no corrections
no plots

when you read this
you will find me

happiness is not
a consolation prize for spinelessness

do you mean that meaning is impossible

is always new

FIGURING IT OUT

What happens, the tumult asks,
when you fall through history?

That's not where the pearl is buried.
Why do I throw parties
in the abyss?

This time I'll paint your password.

BREEDING ARCS

Aftermath
Behind enemy lines
Military response
Reprisals
Seductions of mayhem
Thinning hair
Shadow of lotus
Another way to fail
at measuring the rock bottom

ON THE VERGE

You tore into the monotony
of courtroom and couture Who
cares about grave markers I
am grateful that I've not
stood still for inheritance
or exasperation Let them mind
their business Outcries of
carnations and transitive
parakeets Luck's in a bad shape
It's getting absurder The horrible
stuff is coming down from
the sky Who cares about countdown
clocks Though you may try no one
can master the world All's
hot here Berries betray me

TWO LOVERS

Of the two lovers,
hold the one with
a rectangle.

When will
      these skinny minutes
            put on more flesh?

Somewhere inside brightness
is a doorbuster.

Over crushed ice:
letters of spice
& journals of smoke.

WHAT'S AT RISK OF BEING FORGOTTEN

Fear is something
I've touched and known
only with my hands.

Life is exile.
You lost your way.
The afternoon sets a song on fire.

The sun split the poem
gave one part to anguish
gave the other to our nakedness.

At least, I'm not interested
in I told you so.

AS ANY BANNER

The spaces between the creases
of your face

the layout of embossments

by now you should know
that triangles are sounds
as you flow within

and across me

OF IMPRINTING

When I touch
your spine
or your nipple
may you take
over the green north.
Take root.

The soapboat
with its prospecting
                        year.

Under brambles
a signpost catches fire.
This poem smells
of both of us.

STILL AT IT

There's no death
this earth can't stomach.
What travels with you
                    after death?

The spaces between
his lines between his boasts.
                    Same style same yearning.

Morning running out
                    of light,
running out of battery.

This halo is insane.
                    Too long frenching a crawl

ever since the fiesta
                    and how it turned out.

Still at it with archery cancelled.
Still at it with downsliders.

AND THE MOORINGS

And the moorings of half a word
in a blinding patch
a garden's wisdom and ecstasy
hair flesh rock voice
our necks our legs our hands
naked not hiding the pink guitars
the leather straps ringlets triadic
ringlets if lust breeds celebration
confess secrets when we climax
otherwise whichever route takes
us to the front seats of a car

EVERYTHING YOU NEED

Galaxies to be exact.
Planets in panties.
One stop
and what moves you.
One last thing
and citrus.
Everything you need
to be true to the rock
that rocked your blue-jeaned heart.

SERETITA

Kerneling
you broke echoes
& sang me into a blue sky

I ride with summer
inside your letter

Bongoing
you got loose
& sang me into
a poem & a half
a day

I ride with summer
inside your letter

& the poem takes off her undies

GOOD THING

Everyone burning shade
the jazz that rushed in
without you

of arteries
their sanctuaries

and imprints
that become less important

it's not hard
to have a falling out
with an onion

for miles and miles
you give me every
good thing you can't keep
we ride our agonies to death

RUMBLE

Flinging tranquility
against binoculars.
When to say when
in stone and grass.
In Watts, LA, 1965:
"Turn Left or Get Shot".
It took a while
            for the wound to speak.

FISHING ROD

No hand to hold
on to. Did it turn
out to be a tumult
as such? Roof beam,
fishing rod.

There's no better weather
than this to africanize
                    the lexicon.

TO TONGUE IT

Postcards from the wrong
side of the Law

but not just transcribing
terms of infringement.

It's daylight saving time.
My madness returns.

I want to punch everyone.
I want to tongue
a conspiracy midfield.

OUT OF REACH

The street
I played on as a child.
The violin
you looked for in vain.
Darkness is no excuse
for this loneliness.
(Have you ever been in love?)

RIDING A HONDA

Riding a Honda across
the farms & palmtrees
of Nsukka.

The poem catches light.

Let's unsettle this settlement.

Rooting for chances
with Balaclavas.

The bawd in review.
Bright nomad. No stopping.

Not the end of the line.

TO TOUCH

The orchids in the abyss
of a first page.

To touch is to reverse
the absentmindedness of emerald.

In this circle an eyeflash
                to herald the emerald.

Umlaut, not ring finger.

Caresses repeat
                upon a harmonium.

To pluck a fruit
is to see tattoos fuse with chords.

An ebbing memory
                inclined to singularities.

Back of the hand,
                back of the leg.

ADDRESSLESSNESS

A secret sky.
As if jumping
from a high ledge
into the rain of love.
Asslessness be damned.
Addresslessness be damned.

LINE OF DEVOLUTION

A fish tugs a line
in order to understand
why pleasure is so inflammatory.
I'm a line of devolution. Road out,
long haul, grunt of jackfish.
The sky is still
making love to trees.
Caresses which mount, filled to
the hilt. Flow of clouds. The shine
on leaves. Bark & branches that stretch.
Whichever feeling. Cumulus & roots that merge.
This full stroke. This full swing.

WHERE YOU SIT

Where you sit
and think
your floorlessness is trenchant.

I flip because I can't
stand the seawave
that slams against my syntax.

I thought it was perfect
to punch the scripture
in the mouth.

I tumble and keep
odd hours. Come share
them with me.

Too tempting
are the snares
and exclusions of the brooding mica.

YOU MUST HAVE THE GUTS

You must have the guts
to save this city. To
double-trouble my conversation.

The sun walks too fast
on the south shore.

From a tremor I take my cue.
I'm frantic on the balcony rail.

You must have the guts
to tear absence apart.

I like taking off on my own.
I like taking off my clothes
for no reason.

I don't want to barge in
on a shot in the dark.

TABLE OF NOON

You spread your legs
as you set the table
of noon. Our naked bodies
suck the light to the very
last drop. At the peak
of writing, a blank paper
becomes wet. We take
our hands off the handrails.

WHAT THE CRICKETS SAID

Not babbling.
Crickets reciting poetry.
I did not forget
what the crickets said.
Flowers hid inside pylons.
Not spring.
The world needed the spilt milk.
Take me back
to the cuntflowers of the house
where I was born.

THE BURNING BOUQUET

This radiance of nipples
while a cup licks its wounds.
This daybreak of embraces
while drowning arias to death.
The sharpening flute.
The kneecaps of violets.
The burning bouquet.

A NEED TO CROSS A LINE

Season of a favored house.
Transformation from legend
to mere man. Letters of desire
follow us even when our limbs
are falling apart. Backwoods
and peacocks. Boats of
the boudoir. Walking on tiptoe.
You were going out, I was
going in. A need to cross a line.
In a white suit. Penguin on
a shoreline. Caressing the face
of a kiss. Our first brush
with climax. A dark desk.
A true peak. Plain sense of
departure. Riding on our troubled inheritance.

STICKERS AND LILIES

You are the hard road
that holds open house.
We meet and undulate
in the glare as if to
attack a sparkle. Lips bloom
in a speeding midday.
All the alphabets go mad.
Tattoos boil inside stickers and lilies.
Pollen on breast, nectar on penis.

HEAD TO HEART

I'm not sure
how I got here
You take
and you give
head to heart
patch to patch
our canvases
know each other
heart to head
our colors
know each other
the way to poolsides
of exit plans
they are of
all spaces all places
these streets
go on blind dates

SHARDS OF DAWN

A north wind pierces the tongue.
White aria. Gingko trees of distraction.
I make my way into the arms of trouble
as if I'm in love without a lover.
Blood opens its mouth. Warm fingers
of endless caresses. A calendar dares
the final hour while those arms open
and close. Shards of dawn. Dream glides
along textured flesh. You make sublimity
hot. Crystals awaken to us awakening.

ALWAYS BE TRUE

By the dash light
riding shotgun.
No matter what
always be true
to your contradictions.
May take us a while
to get there.
Always be true
to your idiosyncrasies.
Be extra tender.
May take us a while
to fly blind.
You kicked me
harder than you know.
A bowl of sorrow
in the aisle.
Passing by
my antenna mooning around.
Take it and run.
What you sing sings you
north of the border.

DOUBLE ACT

Solitude & architecture
as verdicts on poetry.

I'm a survivor of the siege
of violinists

& when I'm in a hole
I dig deeper.

Lipstick, boat & labyrinthine smoke.
From rake to romantic, I'll recline.

Is the sofa red? Is the perfume
Chanel?

Cream of the double act. No peach.
No problem.

Keep parting my buttocks
with scented fingers.

OPENING DOORS

I smell you
your smell goes straight
    to my head.
Your breath's on my face.
     We hold our
course through
hyphens and garlands.
     Seed of
the flute. Those rustling
footfalls at
    the deepest point
of the black mass
     of orgasm.

HAWK OF FRACTURE

That transition from jail
to street after the first
season. That moment a bell
began to blink. It might be
interesting to think of
the hawk of fracture
or whiskey weather (wherever
we are.) You can bear almost
anything but hypocrisy. Draft
or veil a wake-up call. All loves
are impossible until the right
lover shows up. Folding
                              up
                                 the straw mat.

MATHS

You jumped into the dream
of a finch

where you were least expected.
As for cunnilingus piano-bred...

I snuck out
to conduct the choir of the underbrush.

Off on another trip
without flags.

Sending a solo
with an imperfect Oud.

Nothingness is full of something.

Sketches which you outlined
from one autoharp to the next.

WITHIN THE TONGUE

Moves with nothing
but floral predicament.

Adjacencies at the edge of a foyer.
Across the board
chance licks your balls.

Enchantment does not erase
mathematical accuracies.

I still think well of the mixing deck.
Chili cliffs of clemency.

Exit/break away.
I can't keep pretending
that I know your secret.

Now that I've filled my plate
can I fill yours?

IN THE RETINUE

How far would you go
for a reboot

all or nothing
   marble & skin

I was flying over Brooklyn
this was not a tease

For better & for worse
   I don't need a protective layer

Not becalmed storms
but the ease with which
you got involved with uninvolvement

thinking it not right
to live up to the myth
    following us around—

skins: gateways: the full leaf of your smile

LONG AGO

A rag on linoleum.
Interior with love.
A sash window
picks up what I'm saying.
With a thistle
I proclaim desire.
Don't split the seen
and the felt.
Let a mirror break the spell.
A black dress
and the unruly laughter
of your hair. Long ago.

BEAUTIFUL ESTRANGEMENT

For you
this is the air
to breathe
because I
was born in the sky
For you
this is the shadow
loaded
with words
and footsteps
For you
this is
the beautiful estrangement
between within us
wetness let loose

WE SCRAMBLE EVERYTHING

Class, ebony & cord.
Ardent forgetting:
voice it & let it go—
wrung/crowned—
odor of flesh
lavish/ravish/coarse touch
goosefleshed & in my arms
interventions/obligations
brightening your tongue
                    & sprig

I'm not sure if
we can be pulled apart:
sequined before a lavender
                    bath—

We scramble everything
just in case the night wants
                    to wet us:

unreconciled but intermingling
                    like mad—

ARMPITS SPINNING

Yesterday
those thoughts
walked through my head
with dirty feet
to evade bad coffee
and solar joy altogether.

They warned me
but I had the good sense
to marry ottava rima.

Armpits spinning.
The growing index
                shuns afterthoughts.

Tangential blue.
Storied delight.
Twitch of calamity.

OPULENCE IN AUDITION

We blow words
in each other's faces.
Yes can do. Even & odd.
A head full
of fantasies of you.
This drive to civility
is slow.
Opulence in audition.
The explorers' bluster.
To close & open to clues
breaking. A flavor of cinnamon.
Troubled preamble.
Curvatures getting warm.
Wind from the west
greedy for speed.

LEGS SPLAYED

Legs splayed.
Lasciviousness
etched to feelings of common decency.

Happy in our own skins
we don't worship
any god of war.

An inhalation.
A drag on objectivity.

To desire
and be desired
behind curtains behind glass.

A XYLOPHONE STUDIES

Drawn to this taste
because it happens
to breathe & because
it is nature seen
through a keyhole.
Our loves run through
our fingers like sand.
A xylophone studies
a ladder of disturbances.

I come to you blindfolded.
I love your ferocity.
Stockings & foliage.

Floorboards.
Naked woman, back view.

THERE'S NO CALABASH

What remains
is sandglass

descending
into a cloud

every borough
is a geography

of terror

each word
is here to burn

solidarity
there's no calabash
to fill with unguents

compulsion
of rubble

BECOMING VISIBLE

Sounds true
like water's anger
becoming visible.

Print & linen
& me
lit by your nakedness.

Purple, mauve
pleasure takes hold.
Why finish a poem now?

CLEAN THE PAINTBRUSHES

The proof.
There are other ways
to look at full lips
full hips.
Clean the paintbrushes
but don't forget
to fall in love.
Turn around
what you made me do.
Everlong in a good way.
I've never
pushed back against ecstasy.

IN THE HARD PITCH

I'm partial
to your Let's see how far
we can push this. Between
the cake and tearing off
our clothes. The nuts and bolts
of synthesizing it beyond
the cutting room floor. A
trainwreck flying first class. It's
back to a shining sky that must
keep its promise to us. A perch
reprised. Up to our necks
in the hard pitch. Truth is:
misadventure is not beneath
our station.
              You know something
                    they don't know.

NOW LET'S SING

All day
the world has been
going to hell.
Now let's sing a
love song.
By folding
I threw the book.
Did I rue the hook.
We're made of stronger stuff
than the short fuses of Wall Street.

MEMORY TORE THE BONE

And memory tore the bone
off the flesh of what really happened.

And the taste of my yearning
got spread under your knees.

And that storm of starlights
took you took me.

Stripped your kiss to the bone.

MY FALL CANNOT BUT BE ANGELIC

For completion
my triumph requires my distress.

Can I be
stopped from rendering the sweet weed?

And love
pushed a crag beyond the point of return.

Purgative at Dam Square
or the apotheosis of the falcon.

As postulates: ultimacy, enginery, intimacy.
At the day's end:

to be with nettle and rose and tulip.
My fall cannot but be angelic.

ECHO OF THE TEMPOS

Every time I turn around
I turn into
your obsession

flirty laughter in the woods

or these poems
from the bottom
of a well

just in case you're
wondering how
to run away
from complexity

echo of the tempos
due to a catch in the study
unless unless we undress
begin to connect to the primacy of questioning
places that leave us give us up
instants the spaces in between
double double whammy

ONCE

Cellists in the tower.
Cellists on the stairs.

& the sky is boiling potatoes.

After dinner
I love to watch you piss in the moonlight.

WHAT ELSE IS BEING SAID

Kiss yourself on the lips.
Let the blood scribble
                    on this foldout.

I want a rematch
          with the deity.

What else is being said
            over the phone.

Where romances wear masks.

At half past eight
when flowers berate bed covers.

STANDING WITNESS

Becomes dirt.
Left to right.
Moves from being
a liberator to being
                    a tyrant.

Becomes cruel.
Like everydude's smoked mirror
he makes assumptions
            he is doing
                        everything right.

The lukewarm
shall never save us.

Standing Rock standing witness.

SLANTED INTO COLORS

I need a hell of a lot
of love to run my life on.
This spine, this patois
this struggle.
A breath divine.
Dream slanted into accent.
Slanted into colors
of the sunset.
On the other side
of those things
I can return to.
To find and hold you.

A RETURN TO BEAUTY

What's a poet
without the gift
of rashness? Tacos
for you and this bony
day. A return to beauty
I have come to terms
with. Sky and its
praise of panties
between chair and flowerpot.
Juice alone does
not define us as you
sit on my face. I've got
my eye on your eyelids,
breasts. Half of a yellow
sun in a state of emergency.

THROUGH THE SENTENCE

As two men with broken skulls, inert,
positioned on the floor,

earthy, too earthy
without jackets, without shoes

in sleet & snow

they buried Schulz & Hauptman
in one grave in Poland

one had red hair
the other had blood in his mouth

what the sidewalk knew
what the street saw

BROWN COVER

Nigerian party? Keep
that rice jumping.

Morning of the imperfect pitch.
Inventory for the pitfalls
of orioles.

Rome in the bone. A blurb
to sink a book

and pluralize a day.

And when I briefly came to your house
you were not bad enough for my taste.

I only wanted to talk to the fishes
in your fish pond.

Prowled the party with a pout.
Tigerstreak at dusk.
Fire to crackling fire.

INSIDE THE LIGHT

You sent me on my way
after many hours
of studying your naked body.

A signature is not only a sign
you said.

The helpless can depend on the helpless
you noted.

You did not broadcast
my conversion,

did not wail Hold Me Close.

I think you have the right
spirit. I just don't know if
the spirit has got you rightly.

THE TABLE WITH A PLATE

I will still be hungry
after my death. I won't
rest in peace on an
empty stomach. A mirror
that blinks is a garden.
Ask it of its yearning.
Capitulation carved into each
grudge while you and the clouds
worship the heat. Needing better
coordination between feet and shoes.

SAMPLERS

They wait for them
to get blown up
        for being addicted to euphoria

stickers of bill of rights
          on windscreens

denials of political murder
          on billboards

They wait
     to pull off
         another secret indictment

an arrow flew into
        your third eye

adamant as
     the denial of nothingness

MUTATION OF HERB

Neither gaiety nor beauty
open wounds singing openly
our history of kisses of gunshots

for bliss is not always blind

was the wrong shape
was the wrong voice
was the wrong fuss
the reading was all wrong too

our ration of the cries
of flight and return

jangling keys fear
the memories of rain
shall be derided

starting point for the mutation of herb

TO RELIGHT A PIPE

Are blacks still trending
this season?

They are classics.

Why for only a season?

Going to give away
the road, hopscotch.

To fool the wind, to relight
a pipe.

Open to the tremor
the stutter of lucidity.

A leap from sadness
to wonder,
markings, latticework.

Accounting, decanting
of the triple experience.

THREE STUDIES

Halfway to squeaky clean image and mistaken identity. Elsewhere:
the full body of a scream. The akimbo stance. Leaning against tiles:
two wet flags dying. Do you need this cupcake by any chance? A
price is chosen. You barter with maniacs of innocence. Surrender
is just a surrender so you tear the travelogue to pieces. Elsewhere:
at the cusp of crisis and hysterical silence. Three studies for a
tightrope. A grenade about to go off. Blood warbling through veins.
Longing for top soil.

GO NO FARTHER

I misread the acrostic you sent. Tomorrow is coming for you. New York ate bread and frost. Open verdict of silver hips. Taking songs from a root to words that died by their own hands. Maybe you will turn up for this one and be heard. Like writing a poem together. That was the way Mark Rothko saw us in his painting. Writing the unself and surpassing belief. Let grief take as much time as it needs around anything that does not leave a mark or something that threatens you. We've had enough of the art of bootlicking.

LIKE A RING

Horses in summer. Secrets of tassels. A stone born of textile. Melody
of coverlets. Excusing the mistakes of a telephone call. Caprice is
expensive. Nights grasp each other when distance penetrates recol-
lection. A thirst for indexing curveballs. Like a ring among rings.
Hurting transitions in between an assignment and walking part of
the way. Life insists on a sweet sheen. There's no blurry balladry; no
lack of paradise. We go reeling. Where you go I go. Monsters of ten-
derness. May we never diminish our mutual surrender. Walking as if
dazzling the crackups of ampersands.

A TOUR

Northbound train
lower level
and the most annoying daylight

as if I could learn
something from
anagram puzzles

mapwork, pulsant
a conversation about it
a tizzy fit

ice cubes, headlines
tough-as-nails midwesterner

pondering the next move
I couldn't stay still

spiraled with a missing letter
shape-shifted with painted pages

FOR THE RECORD

Somewhere between your crotch
and a copy of the Declaration of Independence.

Flee the killer intimacy of balsam.
Meat. Cornet. Oyster staring.

To endure the limning of veracity?
Turn the dirt around! Your nervous
system is an orchestra. The skyscraper
obliges these ruptures.

This is what makes the sublime juicy.
An extreme form of longing.
These close-ups that make mysticism crack.

CITY LIGHTS SPOTLIGHT